FATTY LIVER DIET COOKBOOK

2000 DAYS OF HEALTHY, TASTY AND INEXPENSIVE RECIPES DESIGNED FOR A HEALTHY LIVER | DETOX YOUR LIVER IN A LASTING WAY WITH EXERCISES TO STAY HEALTHY LONGER

BY

SOPHIA L. JONES

Table of Contents

CHAPTER 8. DINNER RECIPES 52

Introduction

STAGES OF LIVER DISEASE

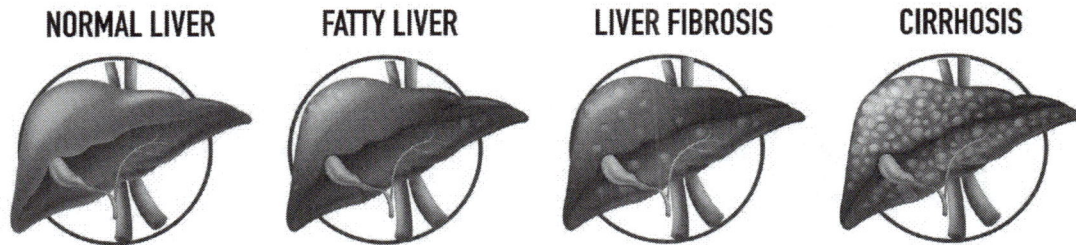

NORMAL LIVER **FATTY LIVER** **LIVER FIBROSIS** **CIRRHOSIS**

This book, the Fatty Liver Cookbook, is an in-depth guide to restoring liver health via dietary and lifestyle changes that are more beneficial to the liver. The nutritional requirements of those who suffer from fatty liver disease are taken into consideration while developing our recipes.

What is Fatty Liver Disease

When an excessive quantity of alcohol is drunk over a protracted time, alcoholic fatty liver disease may develop.

Causes of Fatty Liver Disease

It is a complex disorder that may be actually brought on by a variety of different things. However, some of the most common risk factors that may contribute to the onset of fatty liver disease include the following:

1. Those who are actually obese or overweight have a greater chance of acquiring fatty liver disease than those who maintain a healthy weight.
2. High cholesterol: Having elevated levels of cholesterol in the blood might make one more susceptible to developing fatty liver disease.

Symptoms and Complications of Fatty Liver Disease

In its earlier stages, fatty liver disease often does not manifest any noticeable symptoms. However, when the situation worsens, a person may begin to suffer symptoms such as exhaustion, stomach discomfort, and jaundice.

Fatty liver disease may result in more severe problems if it is not addressed, including liver fibrosis, cirrhosis, and even liver cancer. These issues have the potential to endanger one's life and call for quick medical intervention.

If treatment is not sought for fatty liver disease, the illness might worsen to a point where it poses a major risk to the patient's health. Nevertheless, there are actions that people may do to enhance the health of their livers and lower the chance of getting liver disease. The Fatty Liver Cookbook offers actionable guidance on how to enhance liver health via dietary and lifestyle modifications that are more beneficial to the liver. The nutritional requirements of those who suffer from fatty liver disease are taken into consideration while developing our recipes. We are of the opinion that everyone has the actual right to lead a life that is both rewarding and healthy, and it is our sincere desire that this book will be of some assistance to people in doing the former.

Chapter 1.

The Importance of Weight Loss for a Healthy Liver

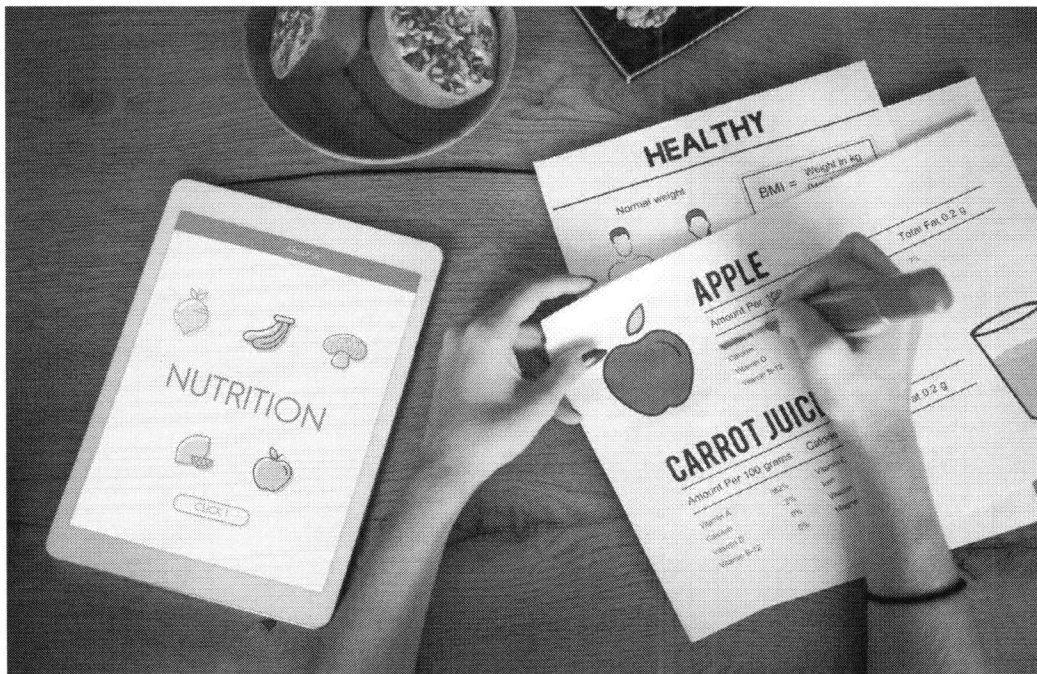

When we ingest more calories than our bodies need, the extra calories are turned into fat and stored in various regions of the body, including the liver. Because of this, one's likelihood of having liver disease as well as other major health consequences is increased.

The Impacts of Excess Weight on the Liver

In the process of breaking down nutrients like carbs, lipids, and proteins, the liver is an extremely important organ to have working properly. When an individual consumes more calories than their body needs, their liver will digest these nutrients and transform them into fat, which will then be deposited in the cells of their liver.

According to the findings of a research that was carried out by the American Liver Foundation, being obese is a substantial risk factor for developing liver disease. According to the findings of the research, those who are overweight or obese have up to three times the risk of developing liver disease as people who maintain a healthy weight for their height and weight.

How Losing Weight Can Improve Liver Health

Losing weight is one of the most effective ways to improve the health of the liver and lower the chance of getting liver disease. When we reduce our body fat, the quantity of fat that is stored in our liver cells lowers, which in turn reduces the amount of inflammation and damage that is caused to those cells.

The Fatty Liver Cookbook offers actionable guidance on how to enhance one's overall health as well as the health of one's liver by maintaining a healthy diet and way of life. The nutritional requirements of those who suffer from fatty liver disease are taken into consideration while developing our recipes, which ensures that they are not only delectable but also straightforward to put together.

In addition to following a nutritious diet, engaging in regular physical exercise is also vital for maintaining a healthy liver and achieving weight reduction goals. The Fatty Liver Cookbook suggests engaging in aerobic exercise of at least 150 min per week at a moderate level. Exercises that focus on generating strength are also essential to the process of gaining muscle mass and boosting general fitness.

The Fatty Liver Cookbook also includes advice on how to lead a healthy lifestyle in order to enhance liver health, such as avoiding alcohol, giving up smoking, and obtaining enough amounts of sleep. These modifications to one's way of life may lower one's chance of acquiring liver disease while also improving one's overall health and sense of well-being.

Losing weight is one of the most effective ways to improve the health of the liver and lower the chance of getting liver disease. The Fatty Liver Cookbook offers actionable guidance on how to enhance one's overall health as well as the health of one's liver by maintaining a healthy diet and way of life. You will be able to actually regain control of your weight and lower your chance of developing major health consequences that are related with fatty liver disease if you follow the instructions and recipes included in this book.

Chapter 2.

Foods to Eat and Avoid for Liver Health

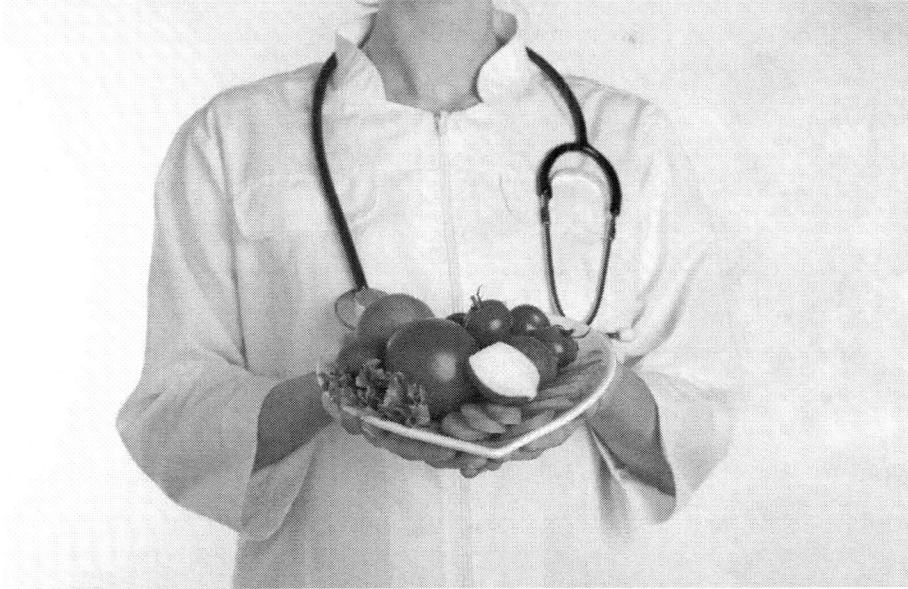

A diet that is heavy in saturated and trans fats, sugar, and salt, on the other hand, may lead to the development of fatty liver disease as well as other disorders that affect the liver. In the next section, we will eventually talk about the meals that are good for your liver as well as the foods that you should steer clear of.

Foods to Eat for Liver Health

Consuming a diet that is both well-balanced and rich in foods that are beneficial to liver health is vital for avoiding or treating fatty liver disease as well as other illnesses that affect the liver. In this section, we are going to actually talk about the meals that are good for the liver, as well as the foods that you should try to stay away from. In addition, we will supply you with a selection of delectable and nutritious recipes that have been developed to assist in the maintenance of optimum health as well as the support of liver function.

1. **Leafy Greens:** These leafy greens are rich in antioxidants, which may help prevent damage to liver cells and are another benefit of eating them.

11

2. **Cruciferous Vegetables:** These veggies also include a high amount of fiber. These veggies have a significant amount of fiber, which may actually assist in the maintenance of healthy digestive processes and lower the likelihood of developing fatty liver disease.

3. **Fruits:** Fiber can also help prevent liver disease from occurring.

4. **Whole Grains:** The consumption of whole grains that are high in fiber content, such as brown rice, quinoa, and oats, may assist in preventing the formation of fat in the liver. These grains are actually an excellent source of complex carbs, which may assist in maintaining healthy blood sugar levels and lessen the likelihood of developing insulin resistance.

5. **Lean Proteins:** The consumption of high-quality protein, which is crucial for maintaining a healthy liver, may be obtained from lean proteins such as chicken, fish, and tofu.

Foods to Avoid for Liver Health

The quality of our liver health is directly influenced by the meals that we put in our bodies.

1. **Processed Foods:** Foods that have been processed, such as fast food, packaged snacks, and also the sugary beverages, include excessive amounts of saturated and trans fats, sugar, and salt.

2. **Fried Foods**

3. **Alcohol:** It is essential to actually limit or avoid alcohol consumption to maintain liver health.

4. **Sugary Drinks:** Sugary beverages are rich in sugar and may contribute to the development of fatty liver disease as well as also the other liver diseases. Some examples of sugary drinks are soda, energy drinks, and sports drinks.

5. **Red and Processed Meats**

In order to protect the liver and lower the likelihood of getting liver disease, eating healthily on a consistent basis is really necessary. The Fatty Liver Cookbook offers a diverse selection of scrumptious and nutritious meals that have been created with the specific goal of catering to the dietary requirements of those who suffer from fatty liver disease. People may improve their liver health and lower their chance of getting liver disease by making adjustments to their lifestyles, such as adopting a balanced diet and exercising regularly.

Chapter 3.

Strategies for Maintaining Progress Over Time

It is a great accomplishment to both lose weight and improve one's liver function; however, the true difficulty lies in continuing to make improvements over time. In order to prevent oneself from regaining weight and going back to having fatty liver disease, it is vital to create healthy behaviors that can be maintained over a long period of time. In this chapter, we will explore the many methods that may be used to keep the progress that has been made over time and prevent the regaining of weight.

1. **Stay Active:** At least 150 min of exercise at a moderate level should be performed each week in order to meet the recommendations.

Finding a workout regimen that one can adhere to over time and that one enjoys is one of the most difficult obstacles that individuals encounter while trying to keep off the weight that they have lost. The important thing is to look for a pastime that you take pleasure in and can easily work into your regular schedule. This might include everything from strolling or jogging to cycling, swimming, or even dancing, as well as taking part in a fitness class.

It is also essential that over time, you work toward doing more strenuous activities. This will make it simpler for you to keep up with your fitness regimen over time and will reduce the risk of injury as well as burnout.

2. **Practice Mindful Eating:** By practicing mindful eating, we can become more aware of our food choices and the way we eat, making it easier to make healthier choices and avoid overeating.
3. **Set Realistic Goals:** It is very necessary to establish objectives that are attainable in order to continue making progress throughout time. For instance, rather of making a goal to lose 10 pounds in a month, make a goal to lose 1-2 pounds each week instead. This will help you reach your goal far more quickly.

When we set unrealistic goals, we are setting ourselves up for failure. By setting achievable goals, we can maintain motivation and momentum, and avoid the frustration that comes with failing to meet our goals.

4. **Keep a Food Diary:** It might assist you in maintaining accountability and motivation to make decisions that are beneficial to your health.

When we keep track of what we eat, we become more aware of our food choices and the impact they have on our health. It can also help us identify patterns in our eating behavior that we may need to change to maintain our weight loss.

5. **Seek Support:** Support can come in many forms, including encouragement, accountability, and guidance.
6. **Avoid Trigger Foods:** By identifying our trigger foods and avoiding them, we can make it easier to stick to our healthy eating plan and maintain our progress over time.
7. **Focus on Nutrient-Dense Foods**

When we focus on nutrient-dense foods, we are less likely to overeat and consume empty calories that provide little nutritional value.

8. **Practice Self-Care:** This might involve obtaining a enough amount of sleep, finding healthy ways to manage stress, and participating in enjoyable activities.

When we practice self-care, we are better equipped to make healthy choices and avoid behaviors that can lead to actual weight gain and other health problems. Self-care can help us maintain a healthy balance in our lives and stay motivated to maintain our progress over time.

9. **Stay Accountable:** Staying accountable is essential for maintaining progress over time. This can include tracking your food intake, weighing yourself regularly, and setting regular check-ins with a healthcare provider or a support group.

When we stay accountable, we are more likely to stick to our healthy habits and avoid behaviors that can lead to weight gain and other health problems.

10. **Don't Give Up:** Finally, it is essential not to give up. There will be times when you slip up or face challenges, but it is important to keep moving forward and stay committed to your goals.

When we don't give up, we can maintain our progress over time and enjoy the many benefits of a healthy weight and a healthy liver. Keep in mind that even the smallest of adjustments may have a huge effect on the way our health and well-being are affected, so every little bit helps.

In conclusion, keeping up the progress you've made over time is really necessary if you want to avoid regaining weight and warding off a recurrence of fatty liver disease. Maintaining our success and living a life that is healthier and happier is possible if we continue to be physically active, engage in mindful eating, establish objectives that are attainable, maintain a food journal, look for support, steer clear of foods that function as triggers, prioritize foods high in nutrients, engage in self-care, remain responsible, and do not give up.

Chapter 4.

Physical Exercises for Good Liver Healing

In addition to maintaining a healthy diet, regular physical activity is another essential component in the treatment and prevention of fatty liver disease. But since there are so many different kinds of exercise, it may be difficult to establish which kinds of exercise are best for the health of the liver. In the next part, we will discuss the various forms of exercise and provide suggestions for seven distinct kinds of physical activity that are especially helpful for maintaining liver health.

Regular physical exercise may provide a number of health benefits, including but not limited to the promotion of weight loss and the reduction of the risk of obesity. It can also decrease inflammation, increase insulin sensitivity, and boost overall liver function. In this particular chapter, we will go through the various forms of exercise and present a list of seven activities that are suggested for maintaining healthy liver function.

Types of Exercise

In addition to consuming nutritious foods and maintaining a regular exercise routine, you may also aid enhance the health of your liver by taking some lifestyle precautions. There are a number of distinct forms of physical activity, each of which offers a distinct set of advantages for your body as well as your liver. In the next chapter, we will discuss the many forms of physical activity and the ways in which they may assist maintain the health of your liver. In addition to this, we will give specific advice for workouts that are especially helpful for those who have fatty liver disease. You may help minimize your chance of developing issues linked with this illness and improve your overall health and well-being by implementing these workouts into your routine.

1. **Aerobic Exercise:** Walking, jogging, running, cycling, swimming, and dancing are all forms of aerobic exercise. Other forms include water aerobics.
2. **Anaerobic Exercise:** The term "anaerobic exercise" refers to any physical activity that consists of brief bursts of intensive exertion, such as running or lifting weights. The development of muscle mass, as well as improvements in muscular strength and endurance, may be facilitated by anaerobic exercise.

3. **Resistance Exercise:** Building muscle and increasing one's strength may be accomplished via the practice of resistance exercise, which can entail the use of weights or resistance bands. Building muscle mass and enhancing one's overall physical function may be accomplished via the use of resistance training.

Recommended Exercises for Liver Health

The liver is actually an essential organ that is involved in a major portion of the metabolic, digestive, and detoxifying activities that take place in the body. Those who suffer from fatty liver disease should make regular exercise a part of their routine if they want to see improvements in their liver health. It has been shown that regular exercise may decrease inflammation, insulin resistance, and the buildup of fatty liver as well as aid in weight reduction. In the following section, we will discuss the many forms of physical activity that are advantageous to liver health. You will be able to increase both the health of your liver and your general wellbeing if you make these workouts a regular part of your regimen.

1. **Walking:** Walking is an excellent kind of cardiovascular exercise that requires little to no special equipment and can easily be included into a person's everyday routine. The overall function of the liver may be improved.

2. **Jogging/Running:** Jogging and running are high-impact forms of aerobic exercise that can be effective for improving liver health. Jogging and running also have a positive impact on overall liver function.

3. **Cycling:** Cycling can also help to improve liver function.

4. **Swimming:** Swimming can improve cardiovascular health.

5. **Weightlifting:** Resistance exercise can also help to improve liver function.

6. **Yoga/Pilates:** Strength, flexibility, and balance are the primary areas of concentration in the low-impact forms of exercise known as yoga and Pilates. These exercises may assist in the reduction of stress and the improvement of general well-being, both of which may have a beneficial effect on the health of the liver. In addition to improving liver function, yoga and pilates are also beneficial.

7. **High-Intensity Interval Training (HIIT):** Intense interval training (HIIT) has been shown to enhance metabolism, which in turn helps to lower the risk of fatty liver disease.

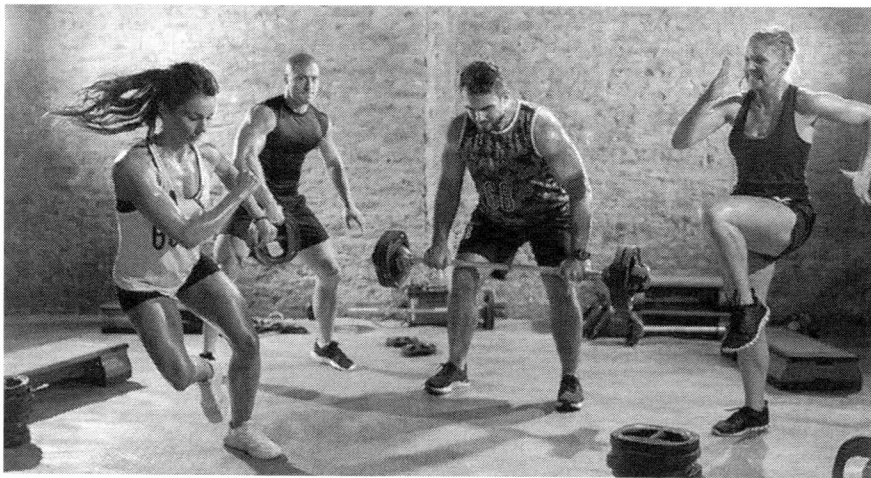

Incorporating Exercise into Your Lifestyle

Now that you already have a better grasp of the many kinds of workouts and the advantages that they provide for liver health, it is crucial to figure out how to include exercise into your daily routine so that you may reap the benefits of these activities.

1. **Set Realistic Goals**
2. **Schedule Exercise into Your Day:** Consider exercising in the morning to get your metabolism going or during your lunch break to break up the workday.
3. **Make Exercise Fun:** Choose activities that you enjoy and mix it up to eventually keep things very interesting. Try new activities or exercise in different environments to keep your routine fresh. For example, you might try hiking in a nearby park or taking a dance class.

As you strive toward leading a healthy lifestyle, take things gently at first, make sure your objectives are attainable, and be patient with yourself. You can enhance the health of your liver and lower your chance of getting fatty liver disease if you are willing to put in the time and effort.

If you want to improve the health of your liver and either prevent or treat fatty liver disease, one of the most effective tools you can use is to make regular physical activity part of your lifestyle. You will be able to develop a sustained fitness regimen that will support your objectives regarding your liver health if you follow the guidelines included in this chapter and select activities that you love doing. Keep in mind that even seemingly little shifts may have a significant effect, and with that in mind, you should begin by establishing targets that are within your reach and then gradually increase both the intensity and the length of your exercises. It is possible to enhance both the function of your liver and your overall health with time and commitment.

Chapter 5.

Breakfast Recipes

Recipe 1:   Avocado Egg Boats

Serves: 4

Prep Time: 15 min

Cooking Time: 30 min

Total Time: 45 min

Ingredients:

- 2 avocados
- 3 slices of bacon
- 4 large eggs
- Freshly chives, for garnish

Directions:

1. Place one egg yolk in each avocado half first before adding the egg white to the avocado (don't let it drop aside the avocado)
2. In a skillet cook the bacon for approximately about 8 min or until crisp.
3. To serve, place avocados and bacon on a serving plate, garnish with chives and enjoy.

Nutritional Values: Calories 220; Carbs 6 g; Fat 18 g; Protein 10 g

Recipe 2: Heavenly Egg Bake with Blackberry

Serves: 4

Prep Time: 10 min

Cooking Time: 15 min

Total Time: 25 min

Ingredients:

- Chopped rosemary
- 1 teaspoon of lime zest
- ½ cup of fresh blackberries
- 1 tablespoon of olive oil
- Black pepper to taste
- ¼ teaspoon of vanilla extract

- 3 tablespoons of coconut flour
- 1 tablespoon of unsalted butter
- 5 organic eggs
- 1 teaspoon of grated ginger
- ½ teaspoon of salt

Directions:

1. Blend all the ingredients, reserving the berries and pulse for approximately about 2 to 3 min until well blended and smooth.
2. Take four silicon muffin cups, grease them with oil, evenly distribute the blended batter in the cups, top with black pepper and bake for approximately about 15 min until cooked through and the top has golden brown.
3. When done, let blueberry egg bake cool in the muffin cups for approximately about 5 min, then take them out, cool them on a wire rack and then serve.
4. Bake in the microwave and then serve.

Nutritional Values: Calories 144; Carbs 2 g; Fat 10 g; Protein 8.5 g

Recipe 3: Pancakes with Whipped Cream

Serves: 4

Prep Time: 10 min

Cooking Time: 10 min

Total Time: 20 min

Ingredients:

- 1 cup of heavy whipping cream
- ⅓ cup of coconut milk
- 1 ¼ cups of ricotta cheese
- 2 large eggs
- ⅓ teaspoon of salt
- 2 ½ tablespoons of swerve
- 1 teaspoon of baking powder
- 1 cup of almond flour

Directions:

1. Mix the almond flour, swerve, baking powder, and salt..
2. Crack the eggs into the blender. Add the ricotta cheese, continue processing it, and gradually pour the coconut milk in while you keep on blending in about 90 seconds, the mixture will be creamy and smooth.
3. Then, fetch a soup spoonful of mixture into the skillet and cook it for approximately about a minute.
4. Serve the pancakes with whipping cream.

Nutritional Values: Calories 407; Fat 30.6 g; Carbohydrates 6.6 g; Protein 11.5 g

Recipe 4: Scrambled Tofu with Bell Pepper

Serves: 4

Prep Time: 10 min

Cooking Time: 35 min

Total Time: 45 min

Ingredients:

- 1 teaspoon of turmeric powder
- 2 green onions
- ¼ cup of grated Parmesan
- 1 (14-oz) firm tofu
- ½ cup baby kale
- 2 tablespoons of olive oil
- 1 green bell pepper
- 1 tomato
- Sea salt and pepper to taste
- 1 teaspoon of Creole seasoning
- 1 red bell pepper

Directions:

1. Cook the tofu in a hot and oily skillet.
2. Add the tomato, bell peppers, turmeric powder, green onions, salt, and Creole seasoning. Sauté until the vegetables soften, 5 min. Stir in the kale for approximately about 3 min until wilts. Add half of the Parmesan cheese and stir for 1 to 2 min until melted.
3. serve.

Nutritional Values: Calories 159; Fat 11 g; Carbohydrates 7.1 g; Protein 10 g

Recipe 5: Serrano Ham Frittata with Salad

Serves: 2

Prep Time: 10 min

Cooking Time: 20 min

Total Time: 30 min

Ingredients:

- Black pepper and salt to taste
- 2 tablespoons of olive oil
-
- 3 slices of serrano ham
- 1 tomato, cut into chunks
- 1 cucumber, sliced
- 4 eggs, beaten
- 1 cup of Swiss Chard
- 1 green onion cut into slices
- 1 small red onion
- 1 tablespoon of balsamic vinegar

Directions:

1. Mix vinegar, pepper one tablespoon of olive oil, into the salad bowl. Add the red onion and tomatoes and the cucumber, and mix with olive oil to coat. Sprinkle with serrano ham.
2. Add salt and pepper, cooking for approximately about 2 min. Pour the eggs into the top. Bake within 5 min, at temperature of 390 F. Serve the salad sliced and served alongside the salad.

Nutritional Values: Calories 354; Carbs 7 g; Fat 26 g; Protein 20 g

Recipe 6: Spinach Breakfast

Serves: 2

Prep Time: 10 min

Cooking Time: 20 min

Total Time: 30 min

Ingredients:

- 2 sweet potatoes
- ½ teaspoon of onion powder
- 2 tablespoons of olive oil
- ½ onion
- Coconut oil for greasing
- ¼ teaspoon of paprika

- 4 eggs
- ½ cup of mushrooms
- Salt and pepper to taste
- 2 cups of fresh baby spinach
- ½ teaspoon of garlic powder

Directions:

1. Oil and heat the baking dish with the prepared potatoes. Season with onion powder, salt, pepper, paprika, and garlic powder to taste. Once cooked, set aside.
2. Bake in the oven for 30 min while turning the sweet potatoes halfway through the cooking time.
3. Heat skillet and grease with coconut oil.
4. Add in the mushrooms and egg.
5. Scramble the eggs.Plate the potatoes and top with the egg mixture.

Nutritional Values: Calories 252; Fat 17 g; Carbohydrates 15 g; Protein 11 g

Recipe 7: Spinach Feta Breakfast Wraps

Serves: 4

Prep Time: 10 min

Cooking Time: 10 min

Total Time: 20 min

Ingredients:

- black Pepper to taste
- 5 cups of baby spinach
- 1/2 pint of mini tomatoes
- 4 ounces of feta cheese
- 2 tablespoons of extra virgin olive oil
- 10 large eggs
- Salt to taste
- 4 whole-wheat tortillas

Directions:

1. Cook the egg in a pan, add 1 tablespoon of oil and then add the spinach, cook and stir often for about 5 min or until wilted
2. Remove the spinach to another plate to cool to room temperature.
3. Assemble the tortilla on a work surface and add a quarter of the eggs, tomatoes, spinach, and feta down the center of the tortilla and then wrap tightly. Repeat the process with remaining.
4. Wrap the burritos in aluminum foil, if you are not using within a week to avoid freezer burn.
5. Microwave on high for approximately about 2 min before serving.

Nutritional Values: Calories 543; Carbs 46.5 g; Fat 24.6 g; Protein 28 g

Recipe 8: Hash Browns

Serves: 4

Prep Time: 5 min

Cooking Time: 35 min

Total Time: 40 min

Ingredients:

- 3 eggs
- 1 big head cauliflower
- 4 tablespoons of olive oil
- 2 sweet potatoes
- Sea salt and pepper to taste
- ½ white onion

Directions:

1. Mix the sweet potatoes, cauliflower, onion, eggs, salt, and black pepper until well combined. Allow sitting for 5 min to thicken. Working in batches, brush a nonstick skillet with olive oil and add 4 scoops of the hash brown mixture to the skillet.
2. Make sure to have 1 to 2 inches intervals between each scoop. Use the spoon to flatten the batter.
3. Flip the hash brown and cook until the vegetable cook and is golden brown. Serve warm and enjoy!

Nutritional Values: Calories 286; Fat 18 g; Carbohydrates 27.4 g; Protein 8 g

Recipe 9: Tortilla Breakfast Scramble

Serves: 1

Prep Time: 15 min

Cooking Time: 20 min

Total Time: 35 min

Ingredients:

- 2 teaspoons of canola oil
- 2 tablespoons of red bell pepper
- ¼ teaspoon of ground cumin
- 2 tablespoons of cilantro
- 1 (6-inch) corn tortilla
- 2 tablespoons of onion
- 1 ¼ cups of liquid egg substitute
- 2 tablespoons of green bell pepper
- ¼ teaspoon of chili powder
- 2 tablespoons of water

Directions:

1. Oil and heat the pan, add the tortilla strips and cook.
2. add the remaining teaspoon of oil. Add your onion, green and red bell peppers.
3. In a small bowl, combine your chili powder, cumin, egg substitute, water and cilantro. Add egg mixture to skillet and cook. Top with tortilla strips. Serve!

Nutritional Values: Calories 151; Carbs 11 g; Fat 5 g; Protein 17 g

Recipe 10: Turmeric Spice Pancakes

Serves: 4

Prep Time: 15 min

Cooking Time: 15 min

Total Time: 30 min

Ingredients:

- 3 tablespoons of coconut oil
- 1/2 teaspoon of turmeric powder
- 1/4 cup of milk
- Pinch of black pepper
- 1/2 teaspoon of baking soda
- 1/4 cup of coconut flour sifted
- 1/4 teaspoon of salt

- 3 eggs
- 1/4 cup of unsweetened applesauce
- Ghee, butter
- 1/4 teaspoon of ginger powder
- Fruit and maple syrup for topping
- 1/2 teaspoon of cinnamon powder
- 1 teaspoon of vanilla extract

Directions:

1. Mix the ginger, flour, cinnamon, baking soda, salt, turmeric, and pepper, and set to the side for now.
2. In a second bowl, mix the eggs, milk, applesauce, butter (or whichever fat you are using), and vanilla.
3. Heat the coconut oil or butter in a pan When it is hot, drop the batter into the skillet in whatever size pancakes you want.
4. Serve with fruit or maple syrup.

Nutritional Values: Calories 178; Fat 13 g; Carbohydrates 8 g; Protein 6 g

Chapter 6.

Lunch Recipes

Recipe 11: Baked Calamari and Shrimp

Serves: 2

Prep Time: 25 min

Cooking Time: 20 min

Total Time: 45 min

Ingredients:

- 7 ounces of shrimp
- 2 tablespoons of avocado
- 1 teaspoon of tomato paste
- 3 tablespoons of coconut flour
- 1 teaspoon of lemon juice
- A splash of Worcestershire sauce
- ½ teaspoon of turmeric
- 1 tablespoon of coconut oil
- 2 lemon slices
- Salt and black pepper to the taste
- 1 tablespoon of mayonnaise
- 8 ounces of calamari
- 1 egg

Directions:

1. Mix the coconut oil and the egg. Add calamari rings and shrimp and toss to coat.
2. Mix pepper, flour, turmeric and with salt. Dredge calamari and shrimp in this mix. Flip calamari and shrimp and bake for 10 min more.
3. Meanwhile, in a bowl, mix avocado with mayo and tomato paste and mash using a fork.
4. Add Worcestershire sauce, lemon juice, salt and pepper and stir well. Enjoy!

Nutritional Values: Calories 368; Fat 23 g; Carbohydrates 10 g; Protein 34 g

Recipe 12: Baked Swordfish with Cilantro and Pineapple

Serves: 4

Prep Time: 15 min

Cooking Time: 20 min

Total Time: 35 min

Ingredients:

- 2 pounds of swordfish
- ¼ cup of fresh cilantro
- 1 tablespoon of coconut oil
- 1 teaspoon of salt
- ¼ teaspoon of black pepper
- 1 cup of pineapple chunks
- 2 garlic cloves
- 1 tablespoon of coconut aminos
- 2 tablespoons of fresh parsley

Directions:

1. Add the garlic, cilantro, pineapple, salt, parsley, swordfish, coconut aminos, and pepper to the dish and mix gently the ingredients together.
2. Bake until the fish feels firm to the touch. Serve warm.

Nutritional Values: Calories 408; Fat 16 g; Carbohydrates 7 g; Protein 60 g

Recipe 13: Berries and Grilled Calamari

Serves: 4

Prep Time: 15 min

Cooking Time: 10 min

Total Time: 25 min

Ingredients:

- ¼ cup of olive oil
- 6 cups of fresh spinach
- Sea salt and freshly grated pepper to taste
- ¼ cup of sliced almonds
- ½ lemon, juiced
- ¾ cup of blueberries
- ¼ cup of extra virgin olive oil
- 1 ½ pounds of calamari tube, cleaned
- 1 granny smith apple
- 2 tablespoons of apple cider vinegar
- 1 tablespoon of fresh lemon juice
- ¼ cup of dried cranberries

Directions:

1. Mix the vinaigrette by mixing well the tablespoon of lemon juice, apple cider vinegar, and extra virgin olive oil. Season with pepper and salt to taste. Set aside.
2. Turn on the grill to medium fire and let the grates heat up for a minute or two.
3. Place seasoned and oiled calamari onto heated grate and grill until cooked or opaque. This is around two min per side.
4. As you wait for the calamari to cook, you can combine almonds, cranberries, blueberries, spinach, and the thinly sliced apple.
5. Remove cooked calamari from grill and transfer on a chopping board.
6. Cut into ¼-inch thick rings and throw into the salad bowl.
7. Serve and enjoy!

Nutritional Values: Calories 567; Carbs 30.6 g; Fat 24.5 g; Protein 54.8 g

Recipe 14: Honey-Balsamic Salmon and Lemon Asparagus

Serves: 4

Prep Time: 20 min

Cooking Time: 25 min

Total Time: 45 min

Ingredients:

- 1 tablespoon of raw honey
- 4 salmon filets
- 1/2 teaspoon of ground black pepper
- 2 tablespoons of ghee
- juice of 1 lemon
- 1 bunch of asparagus
- 2 tablespoons of balsamic vinegar
- 1 teaspoon of sea salt
- 1 1/2 cups of water

Directions:

1. Mix the 1/2 Teaspoon salt, honey, vinegar, and the pepper. Drizzle the honey-vinegar over the salmon, and using the back of the spoon, spread it evenly across the salmon.
2. Place a metal trivet and pour in 1 cup of water.
3. Put the asparagus, the remaining the ghee, 1/2 cup of water, and the remaining 1/2 Teaspoon salt.
4. Pour the lemon juice over the asparagus and fish and serve.

Nutritional Values: Calories 444; Fat 18 g; Carbohydrates 11 g; Protein 57 g

Recipe 15: Lemony Spanish Shrimp with Parsley

Serves: 2

Prep Time: 15 min

Cooking Time: 25 min

Total Time: 40 min

Ingredients:

- 1 lemon, juice and zest
- 2 cups of wild or basmati rice
- 12 whole shrimp
- 2 garlic cloves
- 1 lemon
- 1 white onion
- 4 cups of water
- ½ teaspoon of red pepper flakes
- 2 tablespoons of extra virgin olive oil
- 1 tablespoon of parsley

Directions:

1. Boil water in a pan.
2. Cook the onion, garlic and red pepper flakes in a hot oily pan and add the shrimp.
3. Sauté for approximately about 5 to 8 min or until shrimp is opaque.
4. Add the rice to the shrimps.
5. Add in the parsley, zest and juice of 1 lemon and mix well.
6. Serve in a wide paella dish or a large serving dish. Scatter the lemon wedges around the edge and sprinkle with a little fresher parsley.
7. Season with black pepper to taste.

Nutritional Values: Calories 668; Fat 8 g; Carbohydrates 130 g; Protein 25 g

Recipe 16: Salmon Panatela

Serves: 4

Prep Time: 10 min

Cooking Time: 22 min

Total Time: 32 min

Ingredients:

- 1 cucumber
- ¼ cup of thinly sliced red onion
- 3 tablespoons of red wine vinegar
- Salt and black pepper to taste
- 8 black olives
- ¼ cup of thinly sliced basil leaves
- 2 slices of zero carb bread, cubed
- 1 tablespoon of capers
- 3 tablespoons of olive oil
- 2 large tomatoes
- 1 pound of skinned salmon

Directions:

1. In a bowl, mix the cucumbers, olives, pepper, capers, tomatoes, wine vinegar, onion, olive oil, bread, and basil leaves. Let sit for the flavors to incorporate.
2. Season the prepared salmon steaks with salt and pepper; grill them on both sides for 8 min in total. Serve the salmon steaks warm on a bed of the veggies' salad.

Nutritional Values: Calories 338; Carbs 1 g; Fat 27 g; Protein 25 g

Recipe 17: Seared Haddock with Beets

Serves: 4

Prep Time: 15 min

Cooking Time: 35 min

Total Time: 50 min

Ingredients:

- 2 tablespoons of olive oil
- 1 teaspoon garlic
- 2 shallots
- 1 teaspoon fresh thyme
- 8 beets
- 2 tablespoons of apple cider vinegar
- Pinch of sea salt
- 4 (5 ounce / 142 g) haddock fillets

Directions:

1. Mix the 1 tablespoon of olive oil, beets, shallots, garlic, thyme, vinegar, and sea salt Spread out the beet mixture in a baking dish.
2. Oil and heat the oil.
3. Add the haddock and sear each side for 4 to 5 min, or until the flesh is opaque and it flakes apart easily.
4. Serve.

Nutritional Values: Calories 343; Fat 8.8 g; Carbohydrates 20.9 g; Protein 38.1 g

Recipe 18: Seared Scallops and Roasted Grapes

Serves: 4

Prep Time: 15 min

Cooking Time: 15 min

Total Time: 30 min

Ingredients:

- 3 tablespoons olive oil
- 1 shallot
- 3 garlic cloves
- Salt and black pepper to the taste
- 1 pound of scallops
- ¼ cup of walnuts
- 1 cup of chicken stock
- 1 tablespoon of ghee
- 2 cups of spinach
- 1 romanesco lettuce head
- 1 and ½ cups of red grapes

Directions:

1. Blend the romanesco.
2. Oil and heat the skillet, add shallot and garlic.
3. Add spinach, romanesco, and 1 cup stock, stir, cook for 3 min, blend.
4. Oil and heat the pan, add scallops, season with pepper and salt, cook for 2 min
5. Divide romanesco mix on plates, add scallops on the side and serve.
6. Enjoy!

Nutritional Values: Calories 300; Fat 12 g; Carbohydrates 6 g; Protein 20 g

Recipe 19: Sour Cream Salmon with Parmesan

Serves: 4

Prep Time: 20 min

Cooking Time: 25 min

Total Time: 45 min

Ingredients:

- ½ lemon
- ½ cup of grated Parmesan cheese
- Pink salt and black pepper to season
- 1 cup of sour cream
- ½ tablespoon of minced dill
- 4 salmon steaks

Directions:

1. Mix the juice, dill, lemon zest, salt, sour cream, and black pepper.
2. Season the prepared fish with lemon juice and black pepper, salt on both sides of the fish. Spread the sour cream mixture on each fish and sprinkle with Parmesan.
3. Bake the fish for 15 min and after broil the top for 2 min with a close watch for a nice a brown color. Plate the fish and serve with buttery green beans.

Nutritional Values: Calories 355; Carbs 6 g; Fat 31 g; Protein 20 g

Recipe 20: Zucchini and Mozzarella Casserole

Serves: 2

Prep Time: 20 min

Cooking Time: 30 min

Total Time: 50 min

Ingredients:

- ½ teaspoon of dried oregano
- 2 teaspoons of olive oil
- 400 grams of ground poultry
- ½ teaspoon of dried basil
- ½ teaspoon of dried thyme
- 125 grams of mozzarella
- 1 clove of garlic
- 2 medium zucchini
- 100 ml of vegetable broth
- 1 tablespoon of tomato paste
- Salt and pepper
- 1 medium onion

Directions:

1. Wash the zucchini. Prepare baking dish with 1 teaspoon of olive oil and arrange some of the zucchini slices evenly in the dish.
2. Heat the remaining olive oil in a pan and fry the onion, garlic and minced meat in it until the minced meat has a crumbly consistency. Add tomato paste and season with a little salt and pepper and season with thyme, oregano and basil.
3. Spread part of the minced meat mixture over the zucchini slices. Put another zucchini slices on top and distribute the remaining minced meat mixture on top.
4. Drain the mozzarella, cut into slices and spread on the casserole.
5. Bake for 20-25 min.
6. Take out of the preheated oven, let cool down a little and serve.

Nutritional Values: Calories 300; Carbs 34 g; Fat 4 g; Protein 7 g

Chapter 7.

Snacks Recipes

Recipe 21: Almond and Apricot Biscotti

Serves: 12

Prep time: 15 min

Cooking Time: 45 min

Total Time: 60 min

Ingredients:

- 3/4 cup of whole-wheat flour
- 2 tablespoons of canola oil
- 1/4 cup of almonds
- 1 teaspoon of baking powder
- 2 tablespoons of dark honey
- 2 lightly beaten eggs

- 3/4 cup of all-purpose flour (plain)
- 2 tablespoons of low-fat 1 percent milk
- 2/3 cup of dried apricots
- 1/2 teaspoon of almond extract
- 1/4 cup of brown sugar

Directions:

1. Mix the brown sugar, flours, and baking powder. Add the honey, canola oil, eggs, milk, and almond extract to a mixing bowl. Add chopped apricots and almonds.
2. Bake until gently browned.
3. Keep the container sealed.

Nutritional Values: Calories 75; Fat 2 g; Carbohydrates 12 g; Protein 2 g

Recipe 22: Baked Apples Stuffed with Cranberries and Walnuts

Serves: 4

Prep time: 15 min

Cooking Time: 25 min

Total Time: 40 min

Ingredients:

- ½ lemon
- 4 baking apples
- 1 cup of boiling water
- 4 teaspoons of unsalted butter
- ⅓ cup of chopped walnuts
- 6 tablespoons of grade B maple syrup
- ⅓ cup of dried cranberries
- ¼ teaspoon of ground cinnamon
- ¼ teaspoon of freshly grated nutmeg

Directions:

1. Break off the top inch of an apple one at a time to make a "lid." With a melon baller, scoop out the heart. Combine the cranberries, cinnamon, 2 teaspoons of maple syrup, walnuts, and nutmeg in a medium cup. Stuff the mixture into the apples.
2. To keep the apples, move to a baking dish only big enough. Continue to bake until the actual apples are tender. Serve it sweet.

Nutritional Values: Calories 199; Fat 5 g; Carbohydrates 20 g; Protein 2 g

Recipe 23: Cheese Rolls

Serves: 1

Prep time: 15 min

Cooking Time: 15 min

Total Time: 30 min

Ingredients:

- 1 cup of shredded mozzarella cheese
- 2 tablespoons of water
- 1 large egg
- 2 tablespoons of fresh parsley
- 1 cup of ackawi cheese
- 4 tablespoons of extra-virgin olive oil
- 1 large egg yolk
- 1/2 teaspoon black pepper
- 1 pack of egg roll dough (20 count)

Directions:

1. Mix egg, mozzarella cheese, ackawi cheese, parsley, and black pepper.
2. Oil and heat the skillet. Add up to 4 cheese rolls cook for 1 or 2 min per side. Serve warm.

Nutritional Values: Calories 242; Carbs 25 g; Fat 12 g; Protein 13 g

Recipe 24: Cheesy Mashed Sweet Potato Cakes

Serves: 4

Prep time: 15 min

Cooking Time: 35 min

Total Time: 50 min

Ingredients:

- 1 egg
- 2 cups of grated mozzarella cheese
- ½ cup of onions
- ¾ cup of bread crumbs
- ¼ cup of fresh grated parmesan cheese
- Salt and pepper to taste
- 4 cups of mashed potatoes
- 2 teaspoons parsley
- 2 large cloves
-

Directions:

1. Prepare the sweet potatoes into 6 pieces and drizzle oil.
2. To the sweet potatoes add green onions, parmesan, mozzarella, garlic, egg, parsley and bread crumbs. Mash and combine the mixture together using the masher.
3. Put the remaining ¼ cup of the breadcrumbs in a place. Scoop a teaspoon of mixture into your palm and form round patties around ½ and inch thick.
4. Oil and heat the pan. Cook the patties in batches 4 or 5 per session. Using a spoon or spatula flip them. Add oil to prevent burning.

Nutritional Values: Calories 126; Carbs 15 g; Fat 6 g; Protein 3 g

Recipe 25: Cinnamon Roll Scones

Serves: 4

Prep time: 15 min

Cooking Time: 25 min

Total Time: 40 min

Ingredients:

- 6 tablespoons of swerve sugar
- 2 cups of almond flour
- 1 large egg
- 2 tablespoons of heavy cream
- ½ teaspoon of salt

For the glaze:

- 1 tablespoon of swerve confectioner's sugar
- ¼ teaspoon of vanilla extract

- 2 teaspoons of baking powder
- ¼ cup of unsalted butter
- 2 teaspoons of cinnamon powder
- ½ teaspoon of vanilla extract

- 1 tablespoon of heavy cream
- 1 ounce of cream cheese softened

Directions:

1. Mix baking powder, almond flour, swerve, and salt. in another bowl, mix egg, butter, heavy cream, vanilla, and cinnamon powder.
2. Combine both mixtures until smooth. Cut into 8 wedges and bake for 20 min until set and golden.
3. Whisk swerve sugar, cream cheese, heavy cream, and vanilla. Swirl the glaze over the scones.

Nutritional Values: Calories 156; Fat 15.4 g; Carbohydrates 1.9 g; Protein 3 g

Recipe 26: Cinnamon Stuffed Peaches

Serves: 3

Prep time: 10 min

Cooking Time: 20 min

Total Time: 30 min

Ingredients:

- 4 peaches
- 1 tablespoon of almonds
- ¾ teaspoon of saffron
- 2 tablespoons of liquid honey
- ¾ cup of water
- 2 tablespoons of ricotta cheese
- ¾ teaspoon of ground cinnamon
- ½ teaspoon of vanilla extract

Directions:

1. Boil water in a pan. Add vanilla extract, saffron, ground cinnamon, and liquid honey. Cook the liquid until the honey is melted.
2. Meanwhile, make the filling: mix up together ricotta cheese, vanilla extract, and sliced almonds. Remove the peaches from the honey liquid and arrange them on the plate. Fill 4 peach halves with ricotta filling and cover them with remaining peach halves.
3. Sprinkle the cooked dessert with liquid honey mixture gently.

Nutritional Values: Calories 213; Fat 1.4 g; Carbohydrates 23.9 g; Protein 1.9 g

Recipe 27: Fiery Shrimp Cocktail Salad

Serves: 2

Prep time: 10 min

Cooking Time: 30 min

Total Time: 40 min

Ingredients:

- 1 2 tablespoon of lemon juice
- 1/2 head of Romaine lettuce, torn
- Chili pepper and salt to taste
- 1/2 pound of shrimp
- 1 cup of arugula
- 4 Dill Weed
- 2 tablespoons of olive oil
- 1/2 cup of mayonnaise
- 1 cucumber
- 1 lemon
- 2 tablespoons of Cholula hot sauce
- 1/2 teaspoon of Worcestershire sauce

Directions:

1. Sprinkle the shrimp with salt and pepper.
2. Mix your mayonnaise mix, juice of a hot lemon sauce, and Worcestershire sauce in a bowl. Divide the cucumber and lettuce into four glass bowls. Serve with shrimp, then pour the hot dressing on top. Sprinkle arugula all over and garnish using lemon wedges and dill. Serve.

Nutritional Values: Calories 241; Carbs 3.9 g; Fat 18 g; Protein 14 g

Recipe 28: Grilled Shrimp Kabobs

Serves: 4

Prep time: 15 min

Cooking Time: 25 min

Total Time: 40 min

Ingredients:

- 2 pounds of shrimp
- 1 teaspoon basil leaves
- 2 teaspoons parsley flakes
- Salt and pepper
- 1/4 cup of olive oil
- 16 skewers
- 2 tablespoons of vegetable oil
- 1 clove of garlic
- 1 1/2 cups of whole-wheat dry breadcrumbs

Directions:

1. Rinse the shrimps and dry.
2. Put the vegetable and the olive oil; add the shrimp.
3. Add the salt, breadcrumbs, parsley, garlic, basil, and pepper; toss to coat with the dry mix.
4. Seal the bag, refrigerate for 1 hour. Thread the shrimps on the skewers.
5. Grill on preheated grill until golden, making sure not to overcook.

Nutritional Values: Calories 502; Carbs 31.7 g; Fat 24.8 g; Protein 36.4 g

Recipe 29: Spinach and Brussels Sprouts Salad

Serves: 2

Prep time: 10 min

Cooking Time: 25 min

Total Time: 40 min

Ingredients:

- 1 tablespoon of balsamic vinegar
- 2 tablespoons of olive oil
- 1 pound of brussels sprouts
- black pepper and salt to taste
- 1/2 cup of hazelnuts
- 1 tablespoon of dijon mustard
-
- 1 cup of baby spinach
- 2 tablespoons of extra-virgin olive oil

Directions:

1. Oil the Brussels sprouts, then sprinkle with black pepper and salt. Bake until they are tender.
2. In a dry skillet over moderate temperature, toast the hazelnuts for 2 Min. Move the Brussels sprouts into a salad bowl, including baby spinach. Mix until well-combined. In the bowl of a small serving dish, mix vinegar along with mustard and olive oil. Top it with hazelnuts and serve.

Nutritional Values: Calories 311; Carbs 10 g; Fat 43 g; Protein 14 g

Recipe 30: Spinach Chips with Avocado Hummus

Serves: 2

Prep time: 15 min

Cooking Time: 35 min

Total Time: 50 min

Ingredients:

- 1 clove of garlic
- 1/2 cup of butter
- Juice from half a lemon
- Black pepper and salt to taste
- 1/2 teaspoon of coriander powder
- 1/4 cup of sesame paste
- 1/2 teaspoon of plain vinegar
- 3 avocados
- 1/2 cup of baby spinach
- 1/2 cup of parsley
- 1 cup of pumpkin seeds
- 1 tablespoon of olive oil

Directions:

1. Place leaves in bowls and mix in simple vinegar, olive oil, and salt. Spread the spinach on a parchment-lined baking tray and bake till the leaves are crisp but not burnt, about 15 min.
2. Blend the avacados. Add salt, pumpkin seeds, lemon juice, sesame paste, coriander, garlic, butter, and pepper. Serve with chips of spinach.

Nutritional Values: Calories 348; Carbs 7 g; Fat 50 g; Protein 10 g

Chapter 8.

Dinner Recipes

Recipe 31: Baked Salmon with Garlic Cilantro Sauce

Serves: 5

Prep time: 15 min

Cooking Time: 25 min

Total Time: 40 min

Ingredients:

- 2 pounds of salmon fillet
- ¼ teaspoon black pepper
- ¼ teaspoon of salt, divided
- 1 large tomato
- 5 teaspoons of garlic
- 3 tablespoons of lime juice
- 1 cup of stems trimmed cilantro, fresh
- ½ large lime
- ½ cup of olive oil

Directions:

1. Plugin a food processor, add garlic, cilantro, salt, oil, lime juice, and pulse.
2. Then spoon the prepared sauce on top of the salmon, spread it evenly until coated, and place the tomato slices, and lime slices on top. Bake for approximately about 5 min. Serve.

Nutritional Values: Calories 302; Fat 16.7 g; Carbohydrates 5.4 g; Protein 34.4 g

Recipe 32: Cashew Chicken Curry

Serves: 4

Prep time: 15 min

Cooking Time: 30 min

Total Time: 45 min

Ingredients:

- 2 tablespoons of coconut oil
- 1 medium red onion
- 1 cups of cauliflower
- 2 cups of cucumber
- 1 large egg white
- 1 pound of breasts of chicken
- 2 large fresh tomatoes

For the Garnish:

- minced fresh cilantro
- freshly chopped fresh mint

Directions:

1. Mix the quartered tomatoes, cauliflower florets, and onion.
2. Bake the chicken.
3. Garnish with mint and cilantro.

Nutritional Values: Calories 364; Fat 18 g; Carbohydrates 14 g; Protein 34 g

Recipe 33: Creamy Beef Stroganoff with Mushrooms

Serves: 6

Prep time: 15 min

Cooking Time: 35 min

Total Time: 50 min

Ingredients:

- 1 teaspoon of extra-virgin olive oil
- 1 teaspoon of Worcestershire sauce
- Nonstick cooking spray
- 1 cup of low-sodium beef broth
- ½ teaspoon of dried thyme
- 1 ½ pounds of extra-lean beef sirloin
- 1 medium onion
- 2 tablespoons of whole-wheat flour
- ½ teaspoon of dried dill
- 2 tablespoons parsley
- ½ pound of mushrooms
- ½ cup of low-fat plain Greek yogurt
- 1 cup of water

Directions:

1. Oil and heat the pan. Add the onion and beef. Cook.
2. Add the prepared mushrooms and cook. Stir in the broth, water, Worcestershire sauce, thyme, dill.
3. Stir in the yogurt. Mix in the beef. Serve, garnished with the parsley.

Nutritional Values: Calories 351; Carbs 30 g; Fat 9 g; Protein 31 g

Recipe 34: Grilled Scallops with Gremolata

Serves: 3

Prep time: 20 min

Cooking Time: 10 min

Total Time: 30 min

Ingredients:

- 2 scallions
- ¼ cup of packed fresh basil leaves
- 1 teaspoon of lemon zest
- ⅛ teaspoon of lemon pepper
- 20 sea scallops
- ¾ cup of flat-leaf parsley
- pinch of salt
- 1 tablespoon of olive oil
- 2 teaspoons of butter
- 3 tablespoons of fresh lemon juice

Directions:

1. Blend the basil, scallions, lemon juice, lemon zest, parsley, and olive oil.
2. Put the scallops on a plate. If the scallops have a small tough muscle attached to them, remove and discard it. Sprinkle with salt and lemon pepper.
3. Place the scallops in a grill basket if you have one.
4. Grill the scallops for approximately about 3 Min per side. Drizzle with the gremolata and serve.

Nutritional Values: Calories 190; Fat 7 g; Carbohydrates 2 g; Protein 28 g

Recipe 35: Hazelnut and Cheese Stuffed Zucchinis

Serves: 6

Prep time: 10 min

Cooking Time: 40 min

Total Time: 50 min

Ingredients:

- 1 tablespoon of smoked paprika
- ¼ cup of pine nuts
- 2 tablespoons of olive oil
- ¼ cup of vegetable broth
- 1 tablespoon of balsamic vinegar
- 1 medium red onion
- ¼ cup of hazelnuts
- 1 cup of cauliflower rice
- 4 tablespoons cilantro
- 1 ¼ cup of diced tomatoes
- 1 cup of grated monterey jack
- 4 medium zucchinis

Directions:

1. Fluff the cauli rice and allow cooling. Brush the inner parts of the vegetable with olive oil.
2. Mix cauli rice, tomatoes, red onion, pine nuts, hazelnuts, cilantro, vinegar, paprika, and zucchini pulp. Spoon the mixture into the zucchini halves,and sprinkle the cheese on top. Bake for approximately about 20 Min until the cheese melts. Serve.

Nutritional Values: Calories 330; Fat 28 g; Carbohydrates 5.2 g; Protein 12 g

Recipe 36: Lemon and Caper Turkey Scaloppine

Serves: 4

Prep time: 20 min

Cooking Time: 30 min

Total Time: 50 min

Ingredients:

- 1 tablespoon of capers
- ¼ cup of whole-wheat flour
- 1 tablespoon parsley
- 4 turkey breast cutlets
- 1 lemon
- Sea salt and pepper to taste
- 3 lemons
- 2 tablespoons of olive oil

Directions:

1. Pound the prepared turkey with a rolling pin to ¼-inch thickness.
2. Mix the prepared flour, salt, and pepper in a bowl. Sear the cutlets for approximately about 4 min on both sides.
3. Pour the lemon juice and lemon zest in the skillet. Stir in capers and rosemary.
4. Drizzle the sauce over the cutlets. Serve.

Nutritional Values: Calories 190; Fat 14 g; Carbohydrates 9 g; Protein 2 g

Recipe 37: Paella with Chicken, Leeks, and Tarragon

Serves: 3

Prep time: 20 min

Cooking Time: 25 min

Total Time: 45 min

Ingredients:

- 2 large tomatoes
- 1 small onion
- 2 leeks
- 1 cup of frozen peas
- 3 garlic cloves
- 2 cups chicken broth
- 1 pound chicken breast
- 1 red pepper
- 2/3 cup of long-grain brown rice
- 1 teaspoon of tarragon
- 1/4 cup of chopped fresh parsley
- 1 teaspoon of extra-virgin olive oil
- 1 lemon

Directions:

1. Preheat a nonstick pan with olive oil. Toss in leeks, onions, chicken strips, and garlic. Sauté for approximately about 5 min. Stir in red pepper slices and tomatoes. Stir and cook for approximately about 5 min.
2. Add tarragon, broth, and rice. Garnish with parsley and lemon. Serve.

Nutritional Values: Calories 388; Carbs 5.4 g; Fat 15.2 g; Protein 27 g

Recipe 38: Paprika and Feta Cheese on Chicken Skillet

Serves: 3

Prep time: 25 min

Cooking Time: 35 min

Total Time: 60 min

Ingredients:

- 1 teaspoon of onion powder
- Salt and black pepper to taste
- ¼ cup of black olives
- 1 cup of yellow onion
- Crushed red pepper to taste
- ½ teaspoon of paprika
- 2 tablespoons of feta cheese

- ½ teaspoon of coriander
- 2 pounds skinless chicken breasts
- 1 ½ cups of diced tomatoes with the juice
- 2 tablespoons of ghee or olive oil
- 2 garlic cloves

Directions:

1. Heat the pan Add oil and heat for approximately about 2 min more.
2. Meanwhile in a large dish, mix well pepper, salt, crushed red pepper, paprika, coriander, and onion powder. Add chicken and coat well in seasoning.
3. Add chicken to pan and brown sides for 4 min per side. Increase fire to high.
4. Stir in garlic and onions. Lower fire to medium and mix well.
5. Bake for 15 min, turnover chicken and let it stand for 5 min before serving.

Nutritional Values: Calories 232; Carbs 5 g; Fat 8 g; Protein 33 g

Recipe 39: Portobello Mushroom with Sausage and Cheese

Serves: 3

Prep time: 25 min

Cooking Time: 30 min

Total Time: 55 min

Ingredients:

- 2 Portobello mushroom caps
- 2 ounces of sausage
- 1 tablespoon of melted butter, unsalted
- 2 tablespoons of grated parmesan cheese

Seasoning:

- 1/8 teaspoon of garlic powder
- 1/8 teaspoon of red chili powder
- 2 teaspoons of avocado oil
- ¼ teaspoon of salt

Directions:

1. Heat the pan add oil and when hot, add sausage, crumble it, sprinkle with garlic powder and then cook for 5 min until cooked.
2. Stir in mushroom stems, season with salt and black pepper.
3. Spread sausage-mushroom mixture into mushroom caps, sprinkle cheese, and red chili powder on top and then bake for approximately about 10 to 12 min until mushroom caps have turned tender and cooked. Serve.

Nutritional Values: Calories 310; Fat 26 g; Carbohydrates 6.6 g; Protein 10.7 g

Recipe 40: Salmon with Lemon

Serves: 6

Prep time: 25 min

Cooking Time: 25 min

Total Time: 50 min

Ingredients:

- 1 ounce of parsley
- 6 salmon fillets
- Salt and pepper
- 6 slices of lemon
- 3 cloves of garlic
- 6 tablespoons of butter, at room temperature.

Directions:

1. Cut 6 pieces of foil large enough to wrap around each piece of fish
2. Mix together the butter, garlic and parsley in a small bowl. Place a salmon fillet in the centre of each piece of foil and season with pepper and salt.
3. Make a few cuts in each salmon fillet with a sharp knife and rub the butter evenly among the pieces
4. Bake. Open the packets to serve piping hot.

Nutritional Values: Calories 258; Fat 18.6 g; Carbohydrates 1.5 g; Protein 22.4 g

Chapter 9.

10 Liver Detox Smoothie Recipes

Recipe 41: Apple and Spinach Smoothie

Serves: 2

Prep time: 5 min

Cooking Time: 0 min

Total Time: 5 min

Ingredients:

- 1 teaspoon of ground cinnamon
- 2 cups of almond milk
- 1 banana
- 4 cups of spinach
- 1/8 teaspoon of salt
- 2 tablespoons of almond butter
- 2 small green apples

Directions:

1. Blend all the ingredients.
2. Pulse for 45 to 60 seconds or more depending on the blender until well combined and smooth, and then distribute the smoothie between two glasses.
3. Serve straight away.
4. Enjoy your Apple and Spinach Smoothie!

Nutritional Values: Calories 150; Carbs 6 g; Fat 3 g; Protein 8 g

Recipe 42: Banana Blue Green Smoothie

Serves: 1

Prep time: 10 min

Cooking Time: 0 min

Total Time: 10 min

Ingredients:

- 1 cup of "greens" of your choice
- 1/4 cup of ice
- 1 teaspoon of honey
- 4 tablespoons of orange juice
- 2 tablespoons of blueberries
- 1/3 cup of banana
- 1/4 teaspoon of vanilla extract
-

Directions:

1. Add 1/3 cup of frozen, peeled, sliced banana, 1 cup of "greens" of your choice, 1/4 cup of ice, four tablespoons of orange juice, two tablespoons of frozen blueberries, one teaspoon of honey, and 1/4 teaspoon of vanilla extract.
2. Combine and mix them as usual until smooth.

Nutritional Values: Calories 69; Carbs 10.6 g; Fat 6.5 g; Protein 9.4 g

Recipe 43: Collard Smoothie

Serves: 1

Prep time: 10 min

Cooking Time: 0 min

Total Time: 10 min

Ingredients:

- 1 cup of sweet cherries
- 1/4 cup of hemp seeds
- 1 tablespoon of cocoa powder
- 1/4 cup of pineapple chunks, frozen
- 1/2 cup of mango chunks, frozen
- 2 scoops of collagen powder
- 2 cups of carrot juice
- 1 bundle of collard greens or kale stems removed

Directions:

1. Microwave the leaves add one tablespoon of water.
2. Pour carrot juice, add hemp seeds to a high-speed blender, and add cherries, pineapple, mango chunks, cocoa powder, steamed collard greens, and collagen powder.
3. Process for 1 - 2 min. Pour into the chilled glass and serve immediately. Enjoy!

Nutritional Values: Calories 199; Fat 13 g; Carbohydrates 5 g; Protein 16 g

Recipe 44: Garbanzo Squash Smoothie

Serves: 1

Prep time: 10 min

Cooking Time: 0 min

Total Time: 10 min

Ingredients:

- 1 large cubed apple
- 1 fresh tomato
- 1 tablespoon fresh onion
- ¼ cup of boiled garbanzo bean
- ½ cup of coconut milk
- ¼ cubed mexican squash chayote
- 1 cup of energy booster tea

Directions:

1. You will need to rinse the AGSS items with clean water.
2. Boil 1 ½ Dr. Sebi's Energy Booster Tea with 2 cups of clean water. Filter the extract, measure 1 cup, and allow it to cool.
3. Cook Garbanzo Bean, drain the water.
4. You may add Date Sugar.
5. Serve your fantastic smoothie and drink.

Nutritional Values: Calories 100; Carbs 2 g; Fat 1 g; Protein 6 g

Recipe 45: Ginger Honey Smoothie

Serves: 4

Prep time: 10 min

Cooking Time: 0 min

Total Time: 10 min

Ingredients:

- lemon slices for garnish, if desired
- 1 medium sprigs of fresh rosemary
- ice cubes
- 1/6 cup of honey
- 1/2 large sprig of fresh rosemary for garnish, if desired
- 2 large strips of lemon peel
- 1 tablespoon of fresh ginger root, grated
- juice of 2 lemons

Directions:

1. Combine together sprigs of fresh rosemary, lemon peel, ginger, honey and add 1 cups of water in a small pot. Let cool for 15 Min then strain mixture into large pitcher.. Add the 2 lemon juice and three cups of cold water to pitcher, mix to combine.
2. To serve, pour over ice along with lemon slice and little piece of fresh rosemary as garnish, if desired.

Nutritional Values: Calories 69; Carbs 10.6 g; Fat 6.5 g; Protein 9.4 g

Recipe 46: Green Grapefruit Smoothie

Serves: 1

Prep time: 5 min

Cooking Time: 0 min

Total Time: 5 min

Ingredients:

- ½ grapefruit
- 2 kale leaves
- ½ cup of water
- 1 banana
- 1 tablespoon of chia seeds

Directions:

1. Blend the grape fruit, Add the kale leaves, banana, chia seeds, and water. Enjoy!

Nutritional Values: Calories 281; Carbs 57 g; Fat 6 g; Protein 10 g

Recipe 47: Guava Smoothie

Serves: 2

Prep time: 5 min

Cooking Time: 0 min

Total Time: 5 min

Ingredients:

- 1 cup of baby spinach
- 1 banana.
- 1 cup of guava
- 1 teaspoon of fresh ginger
- 2 cups of water
- ½ medium-sized mango

Directions:

1. Peel the banana and chop it into small chunks.
2. Now, combine guava, baby spinach, banana, ginger, and mango in a juicer and process until. Transfer to a serving glass and refrigerate for 20 Min before serving. Enjoy!

Nutritional Values: Calories 166; Carbs 39.1 g; Fat 1.4 g; Protein 3.9 g

Recipe 48: Lemon and Rhubarb Smoothie

Serves: 1

Prep time: 10 min

Cooking Time: 0 min

Total Time: 10 min

Ingredients:

- 1 1/2 ounces of Swiss chard
- 1 apple - chopped
- 1 handful of spinach
- 1 banana
- 1 peach - pitted
- 2 ounces of rhubarb stalks
- 1 cup of ice
- ½ an inch of ginger
- 1 cup of water
- 1/2 lemon - juiced
- 4 tablespoons of walnuts
- 1 teaspoon of cinnamon

Directions:

1. In your preferred blender, combine all of the ingredients once they're ready. It may be shaken or stirred, then served and enjoyed.
2. Before mixing, cube or chop veggies to make them simpler to blitz. Any green veggies go in last. Lemon, celery, chia seeds, or a tomato slice make excellent garnishes. On a hot day, add ice to make the drink colder.

Nutritional Values: Calories 150; Carbs 6 g; Fat 3 g; Protein 8 g

Recipe 49: Raisins-Plume Smoothie

Serves: 1

Prep time: 10 min

Cooking Time: 0 min

Total Time: 10 min

Ingredients:

- 1 teaspoon of raisins
- 2 sweet cherry
- 1 skinned black plume
- 1 cup of Dr. Sebi's Stomach Calming Herbal Tea/ Cuachalate back powder,
- ¼ coconut water

Directions:

1. Flash 1 teaspoon of Raisin in warm water for 5 seconds and drain the water completely.
2. Rinse, cube Sweet Cherry and skinned black Plum
3. Get 1 cup of water boiled; put ¾ Dr. Sebi's Stomach Calming Herbal Tea for 10 – 15min.
4. If you cannot get Dr. Sebi's Stomach Calming Herbal tea, you can alternatively, cook 1 teaspoon of powdered Cuachalate with 1 cup of water for 5 – 10 min, remove the extract and allow it to cool.
5. Serve.

Nutritional Values: Calories 170; Carbs 8 g; Fat 3 g; Protein 5 g

Recipe 50: Tropical Green Smoothie

Serves: 2

Prep time: 5 min

Cooking Time: 0 min

Total Time: 5 min

Ingredients:

- 2 cups of strawberries
- 2 cups pineapple chunks
- 4 cups of spinach leaves, frozen
- 2 medium banana
- 1 teaspoon of vanilla extract
- 2 cups of frozen mango chunks
- 2 tablespoons of honey
- 2 cups of coconut milk

Directions:

1. Blend the ingredients.
2. Pulse for 45 to 60 seconds or more depending on the blender until well combined and smooth, and then distribute the smoothie between two glasses.
3. Serve straight away.
4. Enjoy

Nutritional Values: Calories 80; Carbs 5 g; Fat 5 g; Protein 7 g

Chapter 10.

60-Day Meal Plan

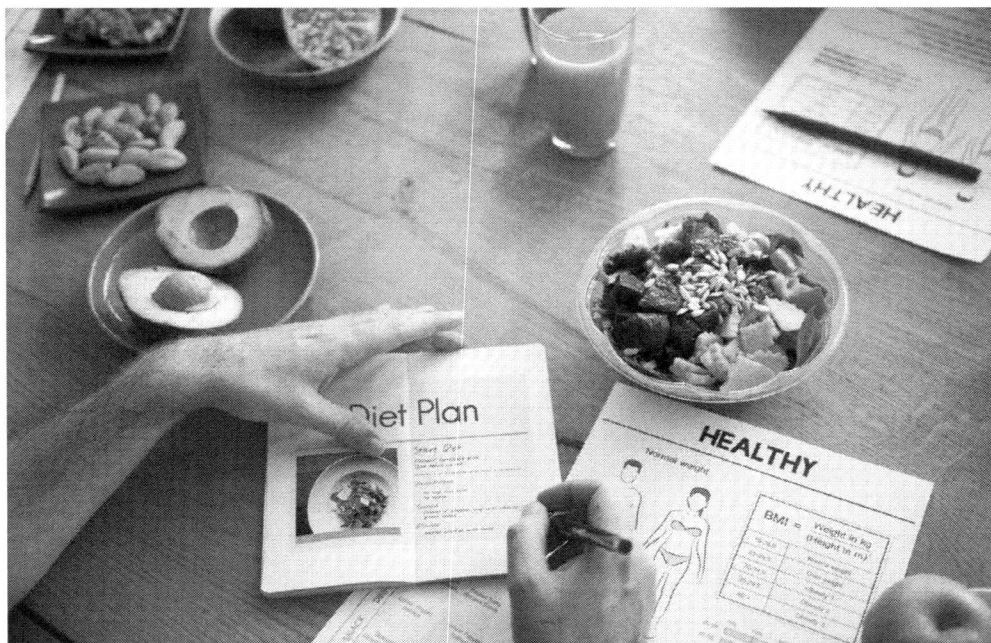

The 60-day Fatty Liver diet plan is designed to help people achieve their health and wellness goals in a healthy and sustainable way. It can also be used for the coming years and repeated for a period of time up to 2000 days in order to maintain constant progress over time. This is because the body needs time to adapt to changes in diet and to stabilize the new weight. In addition, repeating the diet plan helps to consolidate new healthy eating habits and prevent any relapses.

Once the target weight has been reached, it is important to continue to maintain the diet plan but gradually reintroduce all foods. This is because a varied and balanced diet is essential for long-term health and well-being. In this way, it is possible to continue to enjoy the benefits of the Fatty Liver diet plan in the long term while maintaining a healthy and complete diet.

Day	Breakfast	Lunch	Snack	Dinner
1	Quinoa Breakfast Bowl with Roasted Vegetables and Avocado	Grilled Chicken and Vegetable Wrap	Roasted Red Pepper Hummus with Veggie Dippers	Broiled Tilapia with Tomato and Caper Sauce
2	Sweet Potato and Black Bean Breakfast Hash	Baked Chicken Breast with Roasted Vegetables	Sliced Bell Peppers with Guacamole	Grilled Pork Chops with Sautéed Apples and Onions
3	Overnight Oats with Blueberries and Almonds	Quinoa and Vegetable Stuffed Zucchini Boats	Baked Beet Chips	Baked Salmon with Herbs and Lemon
4	Shakshuka with Tomatoes and Eggs	Roasted Vegetable and Feta Stuffed Chicken Breast	Roasted Chickpeas	Garlic and Herb Roasted Chicken with Vegetables
5	Zucchini and Goat Cheese Frittata	Shrimp and Vegetable Stir Fry	Spinach and Artichoke Dip with Veggies	Grilled Chicken Breast with Roasted Vegetables
6	Breakfast Pizza with Eggs, Spinach, and Tomatoes	Grilled Shrimp and Vegetable Salad with Balsamic Vinaigrette	Tuna and Cucumber Bites	Stuffed Portobello Mushrooms with Goat Cheese
7	Scrambled Eggs with Kale and Feta Cheese	Baked Salmon with Roasted Vegetables	Chicken and Veggie Skewers	Roasted Turkey Breast with Root Vegetables
8	Sweet Potato and Black Bean Breakfast Burrito	Chicken and Vegetable Fajitas	Baked Apple Slices	Grilled Teriyaki Chicken with Pineapple and Vegetables
9	Baked Egg and Spinach Cups	Spinach and Feta Stuffed Mushrooms	Roasted Brussels Sprouts with Garlic	Moroccan Spiced Roasted Vegetables with Quinoa

10	Tomato and Basil Omelette	Spinach and Feta Stuffed Chicken Breast	Zucchini and Ricotta Crostini	Ratatouille
11	Breakfast Burrito with Scrambled Eggs, Spinach, and Feta Cheese	Greek Salad with Grilled Chicken	Sliced Pear with Almond Butter	Sweet Potato and Black Bean Chili
12	Breakfast Hash with Sweet Potato, Eggs, and Sausage	Baked Cod with Tomato and Onion Salsa	Baked Mushroom Caps with Goat Cheese and Herbs	Lemon Herb Chicken
13	Whole Wheat English Muffin with Peanut Butter and Banana	Vegetable and Chickpea Stir Fry	Baked Sweet Potato Fries	Roasted Chicken Breast with Brussels Sprouts and Carrots
14	Spinach and Mushroom Frittata	Grilled Chicken and Vegetable Kabobs with Tzatziki Sauce	Guacamole and Carrot Sticks	Baked Halibut with Dijon Mustard Glaze
15	Poached Eggs with Smoked Salmon and Dill	Turkey and Black Bean Wrap	Tuna and Avocado Boats	Mushroom and Spinach Risotto
16	Breakfast Skillet with Eggs, Potatoes, and Sausage	Tuna and Vegetable Pasta Salad	Mini Quiches with Veggies and Cheese	Broiled Flank Steak with Chimichurri Sauce
17	Overnight Oats with Blueberries and Almonds	Grilled Portobello Mushroom and Veggie Kabobs with Pesto Sauce	Quinoa and Vegetable Stuffed Bell Peppers	Garlic shrimp and zucchini Noodles
18	Spinach and Feta Breakfast Wrap	Tomato and Basil Grilled Cheese with Vegetable Soup	Baked Carrot and Sweet Potato Wedges	Baked Cod with Mediterranean Vegetables
19	Avocado Toast with Poached Eggs	Grilled Chicken and Vegetable Kebabs	Whole-Grain Crackers with Goat	Beef and Mushroom Stroganoff

			Cheese and Sliced Cucumber	
20	Breakfast Quesadilla with Spinach and Tomatoes	Quinoa and Black Bean Salad	Baked Artichoke Hearts with Parmesan Cheese	Baked Stuffed Zucchini Boats
21	Smoked Salmon and Cream Cheese Bagel	Chicken and Vegetable Stir Fry	Roasted Acorn Squash Cubes	Moroccan Spiced Chicken with Roasted Vegetables
22	Apple Cinnamon Quinoa Bowl with Walnuts	Grilled Chicken Salad with Mixed Greens	Broccoli and Cheddar Bites	Beef and Vegetable Stir Fry
23	Spinach and Tomato Omelette with Parmesan Cheese	Lentil and Vegetable Stew	Baked Cinnamon Apple Slices	Grilled Salmon with Avocado Salsa
24	Vegetable Frittata with Cheddar Cheese	Shrimp and Vegetable Skewers	Hard-Boiled Eggs with Tomato and Avocado	Chicken and Vegetable Skewers with Quinoa
25	Toasted Bagel with Cream Cheese and Smoked Salmon	Baked Salmon with Roasted Vegetables	Sliced Kiwi with Greek Yogurt and Honey	Seared Tuna with Avocado Salsa
26	Salmon and Egg Breakfast Sandwich	Roasted Sweet Potato and Black Bean Tacos	Cucumber Rounds with Hummus	Grilled Pork Tenderloin with Roasted Vegetables
27	Apple Cinnamon Quinoa Bowl with Walnuts	Turkey and Avocado Wrap	Egg and Vegetable Muffin Cups	Baked Chicken Parmesan
28	Asparagus and Mushroom Frittata	Quinoa and Vegetable Stir Fry	Baked Beetroot Hummus with Veggies	Creamy Mushroom Chicken

29	Cauliflower and Spinach Breakfast Bowl	Baked Chicken and Vegetable Spring Rolls	Sweet Potato and Spinach Cakes	Grilled Sirloin Steak with Roasted Root Vegetables
30	Poached Egg and Avocado Toast with Tomato and Arugula	Chickpea and Vegetable Curry	Cottage Cheese with Fresh Herbs	Baked Chicken Thighs with Roasted Cauliflower
31	Carrot Cake Overnight Oats	Stuffed Bell Peppers with Quinoa and Black Beans	Baked Kale and Feta Cheese Frittata	Chickpea and Vegetable Tagine
32	Breakfast Skillet with Sweet Potato, Sausage, and Bell Peppers	Black Bean and Sweet Potato Chili	Grilled Eggplant and Tomato Stacks	Turkey and Vegetable Meatloaf
33	Scrambled Egg and Vegetable Wrap	Baked Sweet Potato with Black Bean and Corn Salsa	Cucumber and Tomato Gazpacho	Grilled Tofu and Vegetable Kabobs
34	Cinnamon Raisin Overnight Oats	Spinach and Feta Stuffed Chicken Breast	Cinnamon and Honey Roasted Almonds	Broiled Swordfish with Mediterranean Salad
35	Breakfast Tacos with Scrambled Eggs, Salsa, and Avocado	Grilled Chicken with Vegetable Salad with Honey Mustard Dressing	Almonds and Dried Apricots	Stuffed Bell Peppers with Turkey and Quinoa
36	Spinach and Goat Cheese Frittata	Grilled Salmon and Vegetable Wrap with Tzatziki Sauce	Grilled Chicken and Vegetable Skewers	Pan Seared Salmon with Green Beans and Almonds
37	Vegan Tofu and Vegetable Scramble	Grilled Chicken and Vegetable Kebabs with Quinoa	Baked Apple and Cinnamon Chips	Roasted Chicken with Root Vegetables
38	Egg and Cheese Breakfast Quesadilla with Salsa and Avocado	Quinoa Vegetable Stir Fry	Carrot and Zucchini Fritters	Baked Stuffed Eggplant with Ground Turkey

39	Mini Vegetable and Cheese Frittatas	Broiled Salmon with Steamed Vegetables	Baked Sweet Potato and Black Bean Cakes	Lemon Garlic Shrimp with Asparagus
40	Avocado and Tomato Breakfast Toast	Turkey and Vegetable Meatballs with Marinara Sauce	Cottage Cheese with Sliced Peaches	Chicken Fajitas with Peppers and Onions
41	Chia Seed Pudding with Berries and Almonds	Mediterranean Tuna Salad	Mini Caprese Salad Skewers	Broiled Salmon with Ginger and Garlic
42	Breakfast Skillet with Sweet Potatoes and Sausage	Tomato and Basil Grilled Cheese with Vegetable Soup	Sliced Jicama with Lime Juice and Chili Powder	Broiled Sea Bass with Lemon and Herbs
43	Baked Sweet Potato and Egg Cups	Grilled Shrimp Skewers with Mango Salsa	Sliced Cucumber and Cream Cheese Rolls	Roasted Pork Loin with Apples and Carrots
44	Veggie Omelette with Feta Cheese	Caprese Salad with Fresh Mozzarella, Tomatoes, and Basil	Pita Chips with Hummus and Olives	Broiled Trout with Lemon and Dill
45	Cauliflower and Spinach Breakfast Bowl	Grilled Shrimp and Vegetable Salad with Citrus Vinaigrette	Baked Green Beans with Parmesan Cheese	Salmon Cakes with Avocado and Tomato Salad
46	Egg and Cheese Breakfast Sandwich with Spinach	Grilled Chicken Salad	Roasted Cherry Tomatoes with Feta Cheese	Grilled Tuna Steak with Lemon and Herbs
47	Veggie and Hummus Breakfast Sandwich	Turkey and Avocado Wrap on Whole Wheat Tortilla	Baked Zucchini hips	Quinoa Stuffed Peppers with Black Beans and Corn
48	Breakfast Quesadilla with Egg, Cheese, and Vegetables	Lentil and Vegetable Stir-Fry	Grilled Zucchini and Mushroom Skewers	Chicken and Vegetable Kabobs

49	Baked Sweet Potato with Greek Yogurt and Berries	Grilled Shrimp and Vegetable Skewers with Quinoa	Cherry Tomato and Mozzarella Skewers	Grilled Chicken Caesar Salad
50	Cinnamon Raisin French Toast with Fresh Berries	Roasted Vegetable and Feta Salad	Beet and Goat Cheese Crostini	Grilled Lamb Chops with Mint and Garlic
51	Blueberry and Lemon Ricotta Pancakes	Baked Cod with Roasted Vegetables	Roasted Cauliflower with Spices	Baked Salmon with Vegetables
52	Vegan Breakfast Burrito with Tofu and Vegetables	Grilled Shrimp and Vegetable Pasta	Baked Cinnamon and Nutmeg Pears	Teriyaki Vegetable Stir Fry
53	Chia Seed and Berry Breakfast Pudding	Grilled Portobello Mushroom Burger with Avocado and Tomato	Turkey and Avocado Roll Ups	Mediterranean Vegetable and Chickpea Stew
54	Scrambled Eggs with Roasted Tomatoes and Avocado	Baked Chicken and Vegetable Skewers with Teriyaki Sauce	Broiled Grapefruit with Honey	Vegetarian Shepherd's Pie
55	Spinach and Mushroom Breakfast Omelette	Grilled Chicken and Vegetable Panini	Steamed Edamame	Beef and Vegetable Stew
56	Breakfast Quesadilla with Spinach and Tomatoes	Greek Yogurt Chicken Salad with Grapes and Walnuts	Tuna Salad with Stuffed Tomatoes	Grilled Vegetable Skewers with Balsamic Glaze
57	Huevos Rancheros with Black Beans and Avocado	Roasted Vegetable and Feta Salad	Cottage Cheese with Peach Slices	Stuffed Zucchini with Ground Turkey and Quinoa
58	Apple Cinnamon Baked Oatmeal	Stuffed Zucchini Boats with Ground Turkey and Tomato Sauce	Carrot Sticks with Tzatziki	Garlic and Herb Roasted Chicken with Vegetables

59	Omelette with Tomato and Mozzarella	Chicken Caesar Salad with Homemade Dressing	Homemade Popcorn with Olive Oil and Herbs	Broiled Halibut with Citrus and Herbs
60	Whole Wheat English Muffin with Peanut Butter and Banana	Grilled Chicken and Vegetable Wrap with Hummus	Roasted Red Pepper Hummus with Cucumber Slices	Baked Turkey Meatballs with Vegetables

Conclusion

The incidence of fatty liver disease is rising not just in industrialized nations but also in emerging countries, and this is an increasing issue throughout the globe. In the event that this particular condition is not addressed, it may result in a number of catastrophic problems, including cirrhosis, cancer of the liver, and even death. Changes in nutrition, increased physical activity, and weight reduction are just some of the ways that fatty liver disease may be managed and prevented. Fortunately, there are many other approaches that can be implemented.

We have offered in this book a complete approach to the management of fatty liver disease via the adoption of good living habits and modifications to one's diet. We have discussed the reasons for, the symptoms of, and the difficulties that might arise from fatty liver disease. Additionally, we have highlighted the significance of weight reduction and exercise in terms of enhancing liver function. In addition, in order to assist you in making dietary decisions that are beneficial to your liver's health, we have supplied a list of foods that should be eaten as well as items that should be avoided, as well as recipes and meal plans.

It is essential to always keep in mind that treating fatty liver disease is a commitment that must be maintained over a long period of time and calls for patience, devotion, and perseverance. Making healthy lifestyle choices may take some time to show benefits, but in the long term, these changes may enhance both the function of your liver and your overall health. Keep in mind that you should seek help from friends, family, or a healthcare practitioner if necessary, establish objectives that are within your reach, and measure your progress.

In summing up, the Fatty Liver Cookbook is an indispensable resource that serves as a manual for treating and avoiding fatty liver disease via the adoption of healthy behaviors. You may enhance the health of your liver and lower your chance of developing major issues by making adjustments to your diet, including regular physical activity as part of your routine, and committing to making long-term changes to your lifestyle. We appreciate you actually taking the time to read this, and we hope that you have success in improving the health of your liver.

Manufactured by Amazon.ca
Bolton, ON